Else

Mark Goodwin

Else

Shearsman Books
Exeter

Published in the United Kingdom in 2008 by
Shearsman Books Ltd
58 Velwell Road
Exeter EX4 4LD www.shearsman.com

ISBN 978-1-905700-97-4

Acknowledgements:
Some of the poems (or versions of them) in this collection have been published or accepted for publication by the following, to whose editors I am grateful:

Agenda, BBC Wildlife Magazine, Crystal Clear Creators, The Coffee House, Dream Catcher, Envoi, Fin, Fire, Liminal Pleasures, Leafe Press's *Litter Magazine, Masthead, The New Writer, Oxford Poetry, The Rialto, Shoot The Moon, Staple,* Stride Publications, *Stride Magazine, Tears in the Fence, Wandering Dog.*

I am grateful for the following awards:

East Midlands Arts Writers' Bursary, 1996.
Eric Gregory Award, from The Society of Authors, 1998.
Nottingham Trent University M.A. Bursary, 2000.

Thank you to all the members of Inky Fish for years of support and excellent critical feedback.

Thanks to the following for their close critical attention to drafts of this collection: Catherine Byron, Tony Frazer, Chris Jones, Daithidh MacEochaidh, Robert Macfarlane, Julia Thornley.

Thanks to Julia Thornley for proof reading the final draft.

Thank you to my parents, for their being so supportive of my writing.

Contents

For Nikki

SILAS TARN

Silas Tarn's willow-agile feet pick
out a code of stones to step on; he moves
with the slime-ribbony
mood of a river. Those stones under a swirl

of fusion-illumined-'i-hydrogen-oxide feel

as synovially smooth as a newborn's joints.

Silas's legs flicker
a lignin-tensile mesh of muscles. The willow-
yellow of bending motion gleams
under the man-bark of his hide. His arms gesticulate

ligament urges; his fingers glisten
given juices. Silas sweats

hints of sea zawns. His voice boils.

And Silas Tarn's mind is cold clarity over-
lying a deep black dirt. His thoughts
are the wind's doing and ripple only
to the rim of himself—that he slowly erodes.

Silas Tarn's eyes are twigs & water:
a dam that seeps . . .

towards a moment of bursting.

Gravity

4 men & their long dogs
stride through a field's rectangle

the long dogs' sharp snouts cut
air open

4 men release
their long dogs from leather leads

the dogs rocket

and the just-green field feels
the blur of their paws

in a corner of the field
the long ears of a hare are pinned

flat to a geometry
of ghost & body

space is bent by weight
of bones fur & breath

the long dogs fall

straight as light
through a friction of existing

4 men tall & still hold
limp leather leads

with the 5 pronged
stars of their hands

whilst behind the hedge
at the edge of the field

a pale circle

erupts through an unseen horizon

Summer Conundrums of Gladness

happiness hides in ditches
watches
from the edges of fresh-
cut fields

haunts
the square rims
of short-gold-stalked
expanses where hares
patter their terror

happiness hides
in ditches where
waters film with
rancid blue

happiness hides amongst
flesh bones & fur
broken & smeared
over a road
that hunted

happiness hides
in ditches with
death's concise musk

and the sudden exhale
of disturbed
flies

happiness hides round ruts
or potholes
where frog-spawn dries

when sun shines
too long

happiness lingers in each
glass-syllable-lap
a lake makes
whilst herons reflect
into its surface

how their spear-beaks
leave
dark scars on rainbows

and happiness may come
like the scratch
from a cat mad
for a feather you jab
at its claws—

a sudden gleam of
red

how ferocious
fun is
and how happiness
entwines

with sinister smells
& sounds forgotten on
purpose

how sinuous joys frequent
the slow hot

uncoil
of blurred summers

how our wounds
are frilled with
fibres of being
glad

Fathers, Sons & Dogs

My dad lays his dead dog to rest.
His collie the A5 killed.

He's dug the hole himself. I help
him shovel in the dry
summer soil to cover
the paper seed-bag coffin.

The evening light bleeds
gold watery greenness: sun
passing through willow leaves
that hang down—close

to this freshly disturbed soil. We lift

weighty stones
onto the soft mound to mark
the place. The weight of each
is harsh work in moments

lasting beyond this time.

My dad weeps. Utters
unbearable apologies
for the broken dog
he found. He weeps.

Shakes.

I hold him as if I'm a father.

The Widening

the lorry brings   slivers   packed
tight in tanks

where the wet meadow   used to be
a lit expanse waits   a new dimension
for spangled beings   its surface ripples

the driver nets   a metallic fantasy
transfers   sleek packages of virility

from tank to tub   together we carry
a sloshing vibration   to the meadow's

edge

my hands are drawn   into the quivering
inside the tub   a sense as fresh
as teenage disclosures   of touch
or that first   swim whilst naked

slippery musculature   flips & slides
against my arms   as cold wraps
my wrists   I see   yellow-rimmed eyes

wide

my heart pumps   its dark current
and the lake's inside   is wide inside me

the bank's dark soaked   soil smells
cool & full   the driver celebrates
another release with

words

Brookies   *Brownies*   *Rainbows*
and look   a *Zebra Hybrid*!

he describes the finery   of rainbow-fabric
each red spot bears   a blue pin-head

we tip the tub towards   the new dimension
they nose the rim   then

            explode

like knowledge   they streak
soundless   sucked out   by the weight

            of open

Waiting

The sky is ripe—blue fruit,
soft to the sight. The meniscus

of my vision,
bobbing with worldly objects, rests
on two wells:
columns of liquid plunge
through my orbits to my thoughts.

Cool October sniffs me:
a month hunting with autumn. The womb
with much of my fault & talent laced
through its precious mud

is still full.

The sky is ripe—blue fruit,
too big to be eaten. I do nothing.

October's leaves change slow:
show time as cruel as striptease; fling
rusting moments but don't

let go.

Lake water shapes banks. Reeds obey
October: begin
withering. Signs show. I sniff;

water smells of mettles
being polished
to blood's intricate jewellery;

the jeweller, private, showing
nothing, until *it's* done.

Amulet in a velvet bag.

The sky is ripe. This water
is breaking
my impatient heart. I wait,
wait for you; wait

for your charm.

To Adam: Sarah's Surgeon

Adam your blue eyes
sincere as steel met

mine I faced

your gaze like flesh
flinching you could not

anaesthetise I faced
you after you'd been

Adam your blue eyes

after you'd been
with your good-looking blade in

to Sarah's womb
touched

our child before
she was born

Adam your blue eyes
are sharp in mine

when I remember you
my gaze cuts dream

hates yet's
grateful

Ah powerful Adam

Hawk & Toddler

Your toddler's gaze picks out soft
stonework headstoning the telegraph pole
that stands tar-black-straight next
to our house, our shelter, our bolt-hole.

This blood-warm-stone sculpture gazes
through fractal-sifting lenses into a mosaic
of rape-plant volunteers sprinkled across
set-aside. The hawk looks for the to-be-lost.

You point with your little pristine finger:
a fresh soundless word that arrows; pulls
your amazement towards this killer sculpture.
The hawk lifts. Hangs, hangs, hangs. Falls.

Now: The sculpture animated to hard dart
follows its point of existence; drops
onto its sudden find of is-lost; starts
threshing the set-aside's un-harvestable crop.

Winter air paints red on your cheeks,
so, as not-losts, we leave the arenas of cold fields
to their hot dramas; go to our house—seek
the discomforting comforts of the indoor world.

Winter, Feel It

with acknowledgment to
Christina Rossetti & Zoë Skoulding

In the bleak mid-
winter long ago

frost wind moaned
land stood as iron
water was stone

snow fell on snow
on snow on snow

long ago holly
garlands, ivy
smudged red
with lights

in the bleak mid
-winter spring's

fire

*

Winter, feel it—it
bends backs. Dark
thrives. There are

gales. Beneath eyes
bone calls to light.
The moon rolls

out moans, or cuts
her sickle-slivers
of wincing. Winter,

feel it—feel
it fall. Turn

cheek to a too-
small sun to thaw
zero's growth

through veins. Strive.
Listen—under eyes
blood yells. Life's

slammed shut. Feel
winter fall. Rage
is a stone face—stare

at stone. Sharpen
shapes with words.
Learn the greased

curves of roads;
through fog follow
dirtied verges home.

On bright days eye-
trace pylon-lines
against sky across

fields & copses
pewtered to bitter
intricacies uttered

in frost. Trees' still
wriggles tangle
illegible signatures.

Birds call nowhere
by its glassy names.
They all strive:

sleep eat eat eat
sleep eat eat eat
sleep eat eat eat

Some die. They wait.
Winter, feel it. See
light's weight—patient

in icicles' ends, or
scattered on grass
in cold rain.

Fingers

black stars on white sky

five different sized spiders sparkle
darkly on the bathtub's cold porcelain

a constellation of wristless hands stranded
on slipperiness

whenever I find such stars I release
them into arachnid reality
into carpet & skirting-board roughness
or better into the looms
of leaves & grasses where they may weave

with something like solid light

I free them from an unclimbable sky
from smooth existlessness
from this human wash-place's plug-hole

at this moment if I had to pray
the miraculous cosmic mechanisms
of these creatures would do fine for words
they could engineer my superstition
to a clarity of convoluted adulthood
crawl across me as scripture

still my buzzing fears in light

my three year old daughter wants to hold one
one of the smaller stars
she points at her chosen beast

so I lift it from a crackling dry tackiness
a thick itchy breath
its efforts of web on the vertical porcelain

the little wristless hand
of dark star slides
shadow-light

                    from my fingertip to hers
                    across our warm span of bone & skin

she grins glee at the feel
of the crawl's tickle across her palm
up & over her nimble fingers
down the back of her hand

she now knows so well as hers

a wild love moves in the gentleness of her fingers
as the common miracle of this tiny creature
its legs sparkling on her skin

overtly lives

Orange Lilies at the Start of a Storm

thin green dragons of stems breathe
out burning figures

ladies in flames
or Buddhist monks hanged
on Zen green

the sky's plum falls

fat rain collapses to trickle
into mouths at prayer
pious & inflamed

the light green dolphins
of the lily's pods
plumply glistening

suddenly reflect
a white-light-smash of electric

kshhhhhhhhhhhhhhhhhhh

each flame-lady & orange monk shivers
as drops
from heaven bump
their bodies' muffled bells

Sandpit

Sand glistens
on her skin, clings
to her clothes—a summery frost.

She scoops & fills
bucket & cups; measures & weighs; shakes
veils from a blue sieve; tips

trickles or gushes
cup to cup. Countless

grains speckle her palms.

July Storm

She's on my shoulders; her chin snug
on my crown; her hands,
little-strong, clasp
my neck.

My man's fingers & thumbs circle
the glass bones of her ankles.

I am her daddy. Hers.

I imagine the feel of me through
her feelings. She chuckles
at the roughness of my whiskers. I'm the stuff,
in this moment, of her childhood

memories to come: The faint
crispness in the beginning-distance
of her life. These are the days
before her brother will be born.
He is due in August.

These are my last days of this particular

closeness with her. Quickly a glisten

in the corner of my eye builds
to clear silvery wobbles, suddenly pigeons
clap up from the corn, the smooth
heavy-blue sky sheets
electric-flash, her hands cling

a little harder as the dark
clouds rumble.
My cheeks itch with trickles.

As the storm hovers above her she says
with her small-voice clarity,

'Daddy, I won't cry.'

Ways Through an Outskirts Estate

tarmac paths fissured & patched   glass
shattered   plane tree leaves' green-glow
august sun   wrecked

pushchair kneeling in nettles

backs of households   soft
dog turd on the path's verge   a swift

whiff of it knifes
through warm air   windows
doomed wooden with boards   distant

dog-barks   a dog-growl close
behind a creosote-drenched fence   bent
& rusty bmx six feet
up a scorched cherry tree   black

bent-over nails in an oak's trunk   blue
polypropylene rope tied
to a brick tangled
in an ancient hawthorn above

a sickly trickle

in an old meadow-ditch amongst
dwellings that one day suddenly were over this

place   slick wet condom   I step
over a rubber ghost of lust I have to come

close to   a solid ghost

of what can't be stopped from the start
of an animal's evolution   the hot soft

smell of drying

grass-cuttings & petrol   a once-bright
slide swings & climbing frame chipped
& scraped glints
in the summer-sun's blade light   a playground

playground

amongst the enclosed tracts where ways
with names
like Keepers Walk, Shepherds Walk, Thatchers Walk, carry

the feet round these dropped objects   and the body through
this otherside where the wide
car-ways don't go   where the too

clean in smart shoes would take unreasonable risks
with their presences

where eight-year-olds of uncertain
ages wander in strangely dangerous
grubby packs   or hurry

alone

as small as tatty rabbits across

the echo
of a meadow foxes watched   passing adults keep

their eyes to the path

One Season to Another

Louis in his sandpit

briefly he lifts
his head from his play
his dark eyes stare
into sky

it's september
the sky is blue
a deeper blue
than summer's

leaves have
separate tones

the mown
lawn is individual   lit
green blades   not washed
to one plane
by july's high light

september light carries
a warm angular dark

light begins
to glance
a world   as this change

creeps across
earth's surface
and through our air

slow changes
for a moment
are permanent

on Louis' olive skin
each sand crystal
is clear

his hair is fine
bright strands
tight curls
at his nape   growing   each

defined by shine
& shadow

Louis turns   smiling
he stares
into my eyes

Recalling a Little Boy

as a snail feeling
across childhood

travels   a sunset

sinking into a land
whose geology I like   like
childhood

⋆

amongst a tree's leaves
whose sounds
are childhood's thinking

air

⋆

breeze-waves of warm corn give
away invisible childhood's dance

while a cool woodland's dense
with spaces of never

⋆

hair-oil smells of animals   I ask
to be childhood   curl up
in a burrow of my nose
in a grassy bank of my head

⋆

a precise creak
of my breath in

a door-hinge in
a liquid house

I dissolved
a childhood in

⋆

nostalgia clatters a latch

as my first digital watch flicks
childhood-long seconds
into a futuristic

past

⋆

Mum's warm voice joins

in with a crisp wind's searching for me
through long grasses
in a meadow growing childhood

whilst in a corner made
by fields' joining
with a sky wide over childhood

is the well

known secret of my voice

★

childhood-light snowflakes fall

on fallen until
a silence is muffled

★

a word curls
in the ear of my childhood

a word stretches
against the inside of my childhood's throat   through

the mouth of my childhood
a word is a moth with a human heart

a word wonders

Sloe

a sloe's first flavour   shrill

then the clinging-pelt aftertaste   the stone worried
clean of fruit by my tongue   rough
wood-distraction
in my mouth   hedge-nipple   saliva   comfort   my footfalls

on soft rain ground   ah

& the authoritative-chitter of a blackbird   his or her
demand to the demands
of landscape's declaring shapes behind   rising   floating   lines
of mist

hedges moss   fences algae   walls lichen
                                        slopes   this is England

this evening's sky's like
the comfortable threats of a sloe's flavours

(under it I'm tiny
on this rucked carpet of Charnwood   I crawl
through a shadowy weave
of wood rock & soil thread)   my breath

just shows its white
bloom in the cool   a strip of sky brightens

& o a back-lit-birch   my feelings

for *you* are almost dirty   your hairy trailing twigs
long white limbs   black fingers   your pliant
sketch haughty against sky   gods' blissful distress

yet gentle in air   filigree of frail embrace
                                        long sapless grasses clutch

at my ankles   my footfalls
slowed through thoughts

now papery voices of walking
into autumn   my footfalls amongst

fresh fall   perhaps frost-loosened   a layer
of rust-orange beech leaves mixed
with soft green larch needles   a ditch gurgling   a partridge's

feather peppered with water droplets   I touch it   balanced
clear wobbles   mercury-like   slide off   leave
the feather dry

Leicester's distant street lights

to the east   below this Charnwood high ground—
another place   other places   being lit   city (a bowl of embers)
(a king dividing his mind
with thoughts of daughters)   my footfalls painted slow
by mud

in my eye-corner a flamey shadow—
a sudden fox   gone   ha ha a fast hare vanishes   the sun's fall

at first   shrill strands through clouds   then

the deepening into pelt   a huge black oak claims
leftovers of sky   the dark cling   yes   tonight

just before sleep—dream-bloomed black-blues the taste
distinct just beneath

mist

Little Owl

For Sarah

The little owl's call is often perplexing,
even to the most experienced birdwatcher.

the little owl perched
on the telegraph pole
is in silhouette   we embrace

as we watch   share
his wild thrill   the sun's

fading haze enhances
the dark of his shape   he stares

from the dark he is to us

yet his frequenting us
has made him friend

in daylight   watched
through binoculars   his gaze pins
us to our selves

with the severe comfort of truth

his feathers clothe unknown will

his call's a surprise
not a hoot—an urgent
hawk-voice   a modulation

of air so loud   a rising
sudden-
cut-off whistle   briskly repeated

his call's momentarily all
our landscape   distance close

his call's momentarily

all

the summer night is gauze lit
with flittery movements
creatures alive

& the little owl's still shadow
and still the little owl's shadow

until

suddenly he's up—a soft
swoop leaves

a trail of presence

where is he we ask
he's out there somewhere

out of sight
his flight's warm flag hoists

across
our idea of twilight

Budleigh Salterton

alone with early sun   we sit
on a billion pebbles

no seagull screeches   odd
swallows intricately rip
& re-order noise

a skylark enhances silence

sea unshrouds & shrouds
a damp dark band of sound

then they come   feet clop
a dull ring of disturbed
smooth chunks

that have been rounded
by the wet rhythm's rubbed sense

we sit on a billion pebbles   feel
billions' feet not far off

of all pebbles in all worlds
now   fragments of crowd
strangers   choose

pebbles next to us
we're no longer alone
the crowd grows
pebbles around us   makes

us a part

and sea's sound blurs
as the rub

of flesh voices joins noises

Staring at our kitchen's quarry tiles

the red floor tiles jiggle
their solid still

they are tongues cemented
to this raw row with you
my children's mummy

the red floor tiles' corners jab
in my tummy
oblongs viscously swirling brick-up
my thoughts in infinity

the tiles' wordless hardness
tessellates the chaos
the vapours of our sorrow gave
the tiles to translate

the tiles are the beneath of a child's
picked-off scab
they are right-angled red shouts

the gaps between the tiles
are the canyons of our histories
are the grooves of our sighs
are the squints of our eyes

each tile is a key to our fractals of anger
each tile is a key my eyeballs tap
the tiles are the pixels of our crashed program
the facets of a fly's eyes
the bogus turnings of millennia

each tile is a cat
flattened red on a mat

I can no longer stare at the tiles
I can no longer stare at the tiles
as our insults fatten them
and brighten their red

(can I know long smiles of stares again)

so now the table leg prepares
a path
from the tiles to the table-top

of your inexplicable gaze
where hurt cutlery

trickles metal tears

Clones by Sea

A setting sun's reflection-beam thrusts
across sea; pinpoints
a lone figure seeing it. A figure moves,
a beam follows—its dazzling glitter
an only beam; an only one sent
from the sun. A figure may feel chosen.

Another figure a mile down a shore at exactly
a same moment feels a similar
beam pick a face as destination.
A figure may feel random.

Another figure a mile further down a shore, at exactly
a same moment, strips;
leaves clothes, a wallet & identity
card scattered with sand; wades
into cold salt-water; swims into a beam's
glitter until a chill solution cramps
arms & legs. A figure may feel,
at this point, a sinking in to a self.

Frightened in the Gap

rumble of machinery behind hedges
thick walls of summer leaf shaken dusty
metallic whistle-rattle of dozer tracks

same sound as battle-tanks

same iron noise as in war films
of Panzers approaching
relentless across landscape
through houses of cardboard
& woodlands of matchsticks

I walk towards the noise & leaf wall
angry as a man following his bayonet

it is hot but I can't smell my sweat's musk
only burnt diesel's wriggling particles

I crouch and watch
from a gap in the green defence
from within the frail branch barricade
the machines will rip

I could stand

in front of one of these manufactured beasts
matador-arrogant Tiananmen-Square-style

but I don't

pathetically rabbity I watch it happen
the meadow being peeled raw brown
high oaks turned to torn stumps

the ancient in me is petrified
by this tool-violence he discovered by accident
and the modern in me   he is bored of hope

and the me of me   she-he   is stuck

somewhere between them   lost
somewhere amongst their war

I crouch in the hedge alive
amongst live green for the time being   I stare

at the ground's emptiness which used to be a place

which used to be a place

where I recognised my self

I Turned

The lit city's rim is

interrupted: rural pushes
prongs of night through
Leicester's north-western
membrane. I walk

a corridor;
a hawthorn hedgeline here
on the city rim. I'm on

edge,

in the shadows; city lights
are to my right, to my left.

In front earth's dark.

Some blackbird's startled;
sirens reply. The rim

is still in the world

of hard objects; yet rotates
like a circular saw
or some space-station.

I was walking
in the city rim, I turned,
I was walking
along the city rim, I turned.
I follow a prong of rural out

—a space between

I've one boot in grass,
speckled with cow-shit;
one eye alert for bird

vibrations,
or a hare's trace. I've

one shoe on tarmac. A whir
of headlights sparkles
around the roundabout

of one eye's
iris. I'm here

on the city rim.

It's perfectly still
as it spins; I hurtle

off

into damp-grass tracts
gestating menhirs as I'm pulled

in

by the city's
glistening dense

interior. I'm here I'm here

Axe

I lift the seeking weight
let my planet exact
earth's depth
I let it obligate
the waiting mass

then to this potential
I make my addition
I give

some of the power
from the bone & muscle
of the animal I am

so the demanding edge begins
its parting
of the tiny parts of air

it swings

on the fulcrum
of a two-legged
vulnerable & arrogant being

there's a moment locked
in a glint
everywhere forever winks

my palm slips down the shaft's
past of branchness
wood rushes through my loosened grip

the wait

                ing log splits

Peter's Selfless Portrait

My paper is hard dark. Deep
as Said, yet smells of voltage-white;
the tingle of fish slipping. I must whittle

thoughts fish-head sharp before I cut
grey shades of still dance. Inert
motion's waiting to go. Gently

I place

a liquid chisel on my skin; gouge
Nothing's mouth through rock. I'm not
obsessed with Earth's birth-cwm. I *love*.

I love with rain
's hammering pigment; paint
swim's whispery shapes
up my rhyolite bole. My stare must

become tonnes of see-
through soil. But no

artist yet has turned
Stone so it yields to Light's
untouchable glacier. If I fail

my gaze will die before its birth. I will
stretch a yell of Dead
tight & smooth, then paint
it with a pointless breath.

*

My crown's leaves curl
Sea's screams. The chisel
of my blood bit
out whole seasons to rid
mere millimetres
of unwanted medium
from the shape
of Water's claws.
These claws now reaching
for the Moon's dark
& cratered back.

*

Each line along the stone tree of me
has its reason. Here I tear a track
across a moor, and there drip
dots of cairns to pull
a crow from A to B. This trick
in the sleeve of my throat
is a single solid line of song I cough
as snots of lava. As it cools

I sculpt.

Each line is part of dark or bright:
the Sun's rise slices Now, whilst Night's
broken pen scribbles Then. Each line eats

fat & muscle. Each line
's a burning nerve. The river

of my reason flips
back & forth senseless
brushes of fish

*

My face is 13 months of tide.
The black & white I've mixed
through chisels is a pure
illusion of Red. Yes. But

if I could live when I was dead
I'd abandon Stone—cut
my flesh; contrive

a masterpiece of sacrifice. But I'm alive.

Only able to carve
from Earth for my Moon's eye. I cross

the swift red wet
from one salty swollen lip
to the other with tongues

of chiselling fish.

Hard Hoar Frost, January 2001

For N

We wake
to a new world white & shatterable.

Overnight this cold brittle lace grew
to appear in daylight complete
to our freshly opened eyes.

It's as if some anguished artist's
discarded drafts've been unscrewed
to as it happens this—

a brilliance of crazed white pages; a collage
of crinkled manuscripts.

So our old-coloured world now wears
a moonish skin. Yesterday is disguised
with Now's water-dust. Your gaze

is tingling glee; your voice tinkles
an innocent lust: *Look look look!* You're full
of the thrill of a child's suddenly discovering
SNOW.

Glaring black branches clutch
dull tinsels of twigs zag-zigged & saw-edged
with crystals. Trees sport

the white majesty of old men's
heads proudly with the feathery virility of swans;
or, like coy girls, shake
pom-poms of frozen light gently. The sun's rising

suddenly plugs-in

the shatterable world—electrifies
ice hair into wintry
punk-pinks & oranges. A birch becomes
a shivering fibre-
optic rockstar costume; an angel's frame
Bowie could die in,
or his camp peroxide bride. Breezes release,

swirl, and agitate
a big dandruff of Christmas's bits. Whilst mist holds

its silty layers

of glistening orange-then-pink droplets dissolving
on a blade-edge-blue where a moon remembers
its old self faintly. Slowly

the morning-moon's shatterable

disk disappears.

Tadpole Psalm

I

at a lake's rim
in dissolved light
of crystal shallows

amongst decayed
gunge-&-bubble-laden
stalks of last year

black spaces
vibrating pauses
of spring's new sentence
have collected
into floating piles
of impenetrable writing

hieroglyphic
black-spunk mass

II

Her wintered, white hand swirls
a black tangle
beneath
here's air-water border.

Comets awake.
Specks of black come
squiggle.

III

A young beautiful-souled woman says
to a young male lover of poetry,
whom she nurtures in a lake of her gaze:

'Look! black trippy sperm; like
Bladerunner city-scape:
the darting sky-cars
choreographed by gods. Make

your eyes blur—and a teaming
mass, a black mass,
a fertile mass,
a squirming motile mass

widens beyond your mind!'

IV

DARE: hold your head beneath
here's border—let
the black mass eat

the gaze from your face.

V

blackbloodydrops
drip&tricklethrough
thejelly / crystalquim
ofasilverylake

thisrandomorder
ofravenoustadpoles
wrigglingliquidly

baptiseseyes

A Crown in an Alley, July 2001

We are all children of the hedgehog.—Maltese Proverb

Dead-straight. Wide as my arms can

span. A longlong alley between
Birstall's sub-urban back-gardens. It channels our sandaled
footsteps. We're careful

of stingers & broken glass, briars at face-height. Our
torch-pool slowly bounces down
the alley, us
in its robust bubble. The back-
garden fences, high-slatted & private, & night's
sodium-bruised ceiling

tunnel us. Gutter us. Foxgloves

trumpet their shapes, ring visions of bells, rise
from the alley-sides as our light brings
them briefly to day-life. Dandy guards with purple ruffles. Now

in the alley a
perfectly right-angled dog-leg, a square-kink of moment:
the head's compass swirls, cardinals
rotate, our bodies pass

through a glyph-blip in the narrow straight of
this right-of-way. Then

we're bang
on track. Back on line. People
in bed or about to be in their houses either

side of our

movement through night. Suddenly our lit bubble contains
pin-glints
staring at us from frothy shadows on the ground. A gentle
sniffing snout, naked. Now

a ball of darts, a garland
of black-tipped lances.
A hidden head's crown.

We crouch—see fleas like civilisation busy
on a world of spires. With flinching finger-tips I turn
the hedgehog over. I'm curious. Wish
to give our eyes a prize for trying the dark. She's

not totally enclosed. Her
expressive feet give no
thing away. Ferocious
with their vulnerability,
opposing the frightened
aggression of her
weapon-coat. Her belly

invites us to put our desires to sleep. But the alley's boundary

suspended
between
castles of
English
house-holds

moves our bubble along; leaving the hog behind
in the hedge of her night.

Out's Door Dusk

a hoot   from an   other
world makes   a mo

ment's nest   of my
ear a   tawny   owl's

call   plays with   a
light   of a   dead day

Continuing Investigation

It must've been one of the burnt
out cars in the park that rose
to stalk our little girl. Or the oak

along Keeper's Walk, by the pond, charred
at its base, and stabbed
with nails. Maybe

that shopping-trolley in The Brook lashed
out like a rusty net.

Was it some metal figure, buzzing, that burst
from the mains sub-station
at the bottom of Dove Lane? Chased her? Yes,

it must've been an electric touch
made such marks on her.

Perhaps it was the grass grown
long this summer that wrapped
first round her wrists; then

her neck.

Must've been the air, must
've been nothing
that sucked away her voice; pulled
at her, pulled

her away from us. Something
soft & silent & instant & peace . . . The police

have their beliefs.

Map

A piece of polished marble; a slab
easily held in a hand. Though heavy.
Its marbly threads, through greens, conduct
no lies—made of stone it's only stone

these lines convey.

The soft warmth of an un-callused palm
(a poet's perhaps, fingers nimbled on
a qwerty of plastic cobbles) is placed

on this cool green landscape—

the smoothness thrills; for the topography
is flinty rifts & ragged strata
in eyes only. Here's a texture

odd as England.

Eyes keen as a hawk's for mice may
take a long hard look into marble.

Through pond-greens strange lands are profiled:
red-brown coast-lines; hinterlands
of tree-rings; cork-contour vistas. Through all
this dark-red tendrils rivering.

As if, from a trap circling above a globe,
seen like looking down on a world,
this piece of marble, of unknown
provenance, leaves the watcher cold.
Denied as a satellite. Yet the marble's near;

can be touched—touched with a tongue!
But still the taste is the cool smooth
of nothing: The mineral lacework,
delicate as capillaries, is part of marble's
brutal weight: Shut in under gloss.

Such green & multi-toned stone.
A suggestion is—it contains fossil pleasures:
falling moistures & ecstasies petrified.
Visions of smells smokily still.

Devon & Derbyshire have been known
to yield, from beneath their fields, stuff
as odd as this stone. Scientifically—
it's limestone metamorphosed
to crystal under a land's mass. Magic.

Held up to light the marble twists
layers for ages; thready tracks lead down
through silts of kingdoms gone;
the stone filters light—
it can become illumined, can glow

(but'll not be confused with neon
nor transmissions through electro-
cathode ray tubes (though,
it's worth remembering, computers
are electrons flashed through sand)).

The watcher's tempted to take a chisel,
or just a chunk of some
other less exotic rock—to smash

in to the solid pool. Craze the gloss.
Then the crafty polisher's effort
will be lost; the stone inside revealed raw,
the tracks dulled (to follow an effort),
the grain blurred

by rough cracking—but jagged enough
to blood a hand's knuckles. To hurt poets.

Lewis

I

Lewis is
a puzzle
of peat
& igneous
words

skys eag round

interlock
blur

bare
utterances
of moor roll
away

to bruised
hill

-outlines layered

over each
other receding
to faint &
fainter

echo

II

Lewis stains
my mouth
with colours
a peat-cutter's
hands touch

as I try
sounds
of ground
-shapes

but noise

too dark
& fibrous

grows
over

my tongue

III

at Callanish
I walk into a mouth
centred by

a tall tongue

teeth
stand around me

I cannot digest
this island's stripes

layers
dark & light locked
into stones

this mouth's sound
is silent in mine

IV

so heather's
wire text
scrubbing
my puzzler's boots

is indisting
-uishable from smooth

cool mist of gone

condensing
a voice's moisture

on my illiterate
skin

Bangs

for Russ

I

My brother lights his row of fireworks.

His yearly winter tradition when he visits
England's middle. His home now is Falmouth

where the bright ground is close   to the sea's dark,
where the ground's dark is close   to the bright sea.

II

My brother lights
his row of fireworks one

by one. Lights
ejaculate. His dark

frame tos
& fros through dark:

from light

-ing the touch paper to
escaping to distance's safety.

III

fire / ground's touch \ dark
fire / sky's cold air \ dark
fire / our lives \ dark
*
bang
*
bang
*
bang

IV

Each bang evaporates then condenses across
the land around

my & my
brother's childhood home. Each bang's wrinkles

of echo & the silk
of its distance-

seeking squeak settle

in amongst every detail. This shimmer
of noise rubs

against & wraps
around trees & hedges: etches

them, echoes them; hangs
its vibrating molecular fabric

on twigs, grasses, barbed-wire.
These strands & veils

of sound waver
in a breeze that's Time; and they're breathed

by nocturnal & sleeping creatures:
sheep with gongs of dew in their wool, startled;

and foxes with whiskers stringing
the guitars of the rabbit holes

they sniff. These unseen

creatures, & the people, & the houses
of Ullesthorpe a mile or more

away are flashed

across our minds through
eyes of sound. The lake,

a sonic mirror, a sheet
of drenched decibels

that backdrops my brother's display,
its brim dripping

sloshes made by waterbirds,
is a silver then dark

is a silver then dark
is a silver then dark

voice cradled in the mouth
of this land sounding us

out

V

this bonfire's smoke
sings
sharp particles of memory
in our throats

        this scent
        of cordite rings
        the bells
        of our nostrils

VI

bangs begin
as end
in same
extend
in same
contain
bangs end
as begin

word
we give:
reverberation
meaning
we take:
senseless
as infinity
yet the sense
-ation

is a skin
each of our skins

covering everything

the hidden
land & its shapes
in shadows

is a body
each of our bodies

that each explosion skins

VII

My brother has run out of wicks. Dad hands
him an ember-ended stick from our fire.

In the dark a gold-orange glow floats held
by the solid shadow of my brother's hand.

He is a magician of love. A blacked-out actor
serving to us, his audience, an honest illusion.

He is not in the whites & stripes of his day-time
chef's uniform. We see him wear the night.

He is a chef of wishes. He cooks up lights & sounds
in the homely kitchen of the dark meadow.

Each flashed taste & fragrance of sound is seasoned
with distances & inexplicable tangs of human hope.

Briefly, vibrantly, before he lights each firework
a glow grows & rotates as he swings the twig

through the cold air its ember-end is capable of burning.

VIII

My brother lights his row of fireworks.
And the stars are just as near
as they are far. He is just as in the dark
as he is bright. Each bang pulls

our ghosts out: stretches

them tight across the miles of our lives.

The Idea of Entropy at Falmouth

i.m. Peter Redgrove

The peninsula on which Britain pirouettes

is altered.

Falmouth's colours through light are similar
to before, perhaps still
the same. The sea's ticks & sweeps
into the bays perhaps still
as bee-bright & salt-sweet. But to see

at Falmouth is slightly

altered.

A million computers would melt & blacken attempting
to calculate the alteration.
Perhaps the force of gravity at Falmouth
is now slightly less. Perhaps the moon
has slipped some sub-atomic but quantum width
from where she usually is. This alteration

is barely perceptible.
This is because the alteration

is vast.

*

suddenly water without a cup
it can't be contained
it seeps

but has soaked
into all it touched

*

On the thin hyper-real roadmap
of a billion-layered green island
(once termed Merddin's Precinct)

Oedipal eyes still gaze
into dead-ends of measurements,
page-flat faces reflect
copies of copies of copies of copies of . . . whilst

bones & flesh & blood
of a human who pulled

words through worlds
worlds through words

is taken to be spread by ground
by water
by moon
by universe

Double Seal at A Land's Start

A Cornwall, for there is more
than one, places eroded

mountain-blocks against
a January sea's back &

forth shift of cold water. A

seal-pair linger amongst white
brine's sprayed breaths; twig

-thick whiskers electric through
crystal-laden mist. Salt-dew

beads blunt blubber-blooms
of seals' faces. Across

black & marmalade granite brine,
through ozone, squeaks

& crunches. A duo
of seals levitates nocturnal

depths. Seals'

opaque polished disks beseech
their seeing: suck

the light of my landlubber's love
into a shock

-ingly cold beautiful depth. A double
act, a seal couple of

oblong mutt-snouts periscopes sniffs
of curiosity. Perhaps seals covet

my legs' agile locomotion over rocks. I
covet a slippery

erotic grace of seals' twizzling
through deadly glass.

Full Moonrise over Merthen Point, West Penwith

Night's dark-blue fur has brushed
against us as our feet read
a Braille strung
out as path through gorse & bracken that brought
us to this space of time to gaze
back at Merddin's finger poking sea.

Before this night-pelt touched
us, dusk showered
its dim grains through
oak-leaves as we followed
a long grove & its filament of stream down
to the granite coast & clifftop-path. Now

sky's black/blue cloud-layers, peacefully violent, break
& dissolve

            around a green moon

whose ragged metal ingot slowly resolves
her perfect circle; mints
her nocturnal tender; then casts
her crimp-beam across
sea's scare-blue layers. Across

dark-wet parchment she has written
translucent bones: a wriggle-mesh

of gleaming skeletons. Now the headland ends

in chess pieces or granite galleons projecting stretched
shadows on salt where her bone-beam backlights.

A full moon
has made
sea a stage.
Our gazes

follow

a boat's light
passing over
black/blue fright
until
moonlight makes
the boat-shape
dazzle blackly.
The craft floats

its revealed dress
briefly through
her beam's width.
Then gone.

Its part
played.
Back

to being a spot of huddling photons on dark. The diagonal

skyline of the headland juts
tors; moonshine condenses
on their edges. St Loy's Crag is

a faint metallic cream curdling
on shadows; a crashed
spacecraft cooling; or a knight's armour shattered.

To you the moon
is orange, its beam
red fibres wriggling;
but I see greens.

So we talk

of men's & women's
sight—the differences
& red/green colour
blindness. We lie

down together to feel
bright touchless drops of stars rain
down their stillness. We make

our gazes follow (but not measure)
the, as you call them, 'mad', precise-straight
trajectories of satellites: white hot points,
each like a surgeon's laser,

crisply passing across

sky's photon-freckled & stretched

dark blue smooth skin . . .

An Idea of Fire, West Penwith

Fire is my brother's mistress. (So he says.)

Tonight, through her, as chef, he will conjure
the hot of curry for our mouths & stomachs. He will pull
a meal out of the camping-field

that we will eat

in front of his mistress glowing
in our faces, the dark gathering
at our four backs, the stars white
hot-specks light-years above our scalps.

Whilst she dances
scarlet & orange & yellow & magenta & blue wriggling-hot
as Salome she will eat

the air. And because of the dark
that will gather at our backs, and surround us,
her song
of lit colours will be all the more rich.

First my brother begins a little grave: he turfs
the sward, and to contain
his flickering slut he surrounds
the brown earth-mouth with grave granite—
a wall of Cornish stone-teeth. Then he lays

the fire, the stuff of his fire to be, he puts
wood in the hole, closes
the ground with dried grasses & twigs. He is a purist:

his ceremony has no place
for paper, and he must set
her alight with only one strike.

So he pulls out
his single tiny penis—the stiff pink-bulbed match;
with it he scratches
one of the Cornish granites (with England's

Glory). Lo & behold

his mistress begins
at the tip which he tickles
the dried grasses with. My brother takes
a one gasp & then gives
a one long puff back: he feeds
her smokiness with his breath. And now she takes
hold of the grass-hair of the corpse she will bring
to lit life.

My brother's pot of spices
will also come to life, come
to our lives, tease
our mouths with taste-flames, give
weight to our stomachs. My brother's mistress

begins her mesmeric dance. She wallows
in her searing fluidity. Despite

my brother's profession
having blessed him
with heat-tolerant fingerprints he is careful
of her touch as he adds

the smut blacks
of charcoals that are like solid fragments of night (dark
offerings that will enhance her).

All four of us, whether woman or man, as we feel
her heat press our faces, are afraid of

and in love with her, & her dance . . .

Land Send

A cross

of promised-forgotten roots
its igneous mass
through a headland to a black

zawn: A room

of no-human-builder
administering scripted
quivers where fish

multiply frozen motions through

nocturnal depths. Citrus

magma blocks lust's
molecular froth, then rings
as ocean's vast contracts
a granite's chasm. A pebble

-government under
melt/freeze clatters. A sizzle
is exhaled solid. Seals
linger on a breath, above
weeds' wriggling legends, where
salt souls slide

across.

Dictionary
Our block of words once broke open. So vast

A fish-bit turned in revolving wash careers
through a glass movement of yesterday.
A blue declaration rips
shores into statements of crushed shells.

was our rivering ink it swelled across

A, reader, dear ear,
can you smell

three separately connected black
specks? Pert
as Braille's dark flavours?

all page-faces gazing at us. A mass

Crystals bite at eyes
with sky's philosophies. Marmalade

-stone holds

citrus magma still. Blocks
above grow green lichen-beards; below,

by sea, a black of ozone's kisses streaks
a granite's told-like-gold harvest.

And smaller blocks of tilted wisdoms
jumble along petticoat-edges of fields.

of signs—antish & fast. Noise grew its loss

Within a curling luminous blue an amber
-brown herringbone skeleton. Small
but dense as a thought.

A bit of fish twizzled. Some word
before voice.

across our banks of knowledge. Slick-with-rage

A ropeless naked girl drenched
in black motion. Whilst a shame-faced dressed

man, placing metal charms in cracks,
attaches his elastic line of nylon. (A climber.) But

his skin's stretched pupil does
slowly learn naked's visit.

blackorange hardsoft fleshrock

person&stone meltfreeze through

single multiplicities of dance

As down a headland some old
volcano ejaculated solid
golden rooms of no-human builders. A land spins

on a granite tip. Britain
pirouettes.

voice-parts then wore all sorts of dark costumes
to shape the ways a tongue can work a page.

A cottage
on a pelvic

cliff. Red
door frame,
black door.

White spray
through air.
Raw noise.

Words spin
a cross
on a granny's
night-hushed
casement.

On a bed
of bone
an old doll.

Dry slot
& sock-tits,
but skinned
& moist

with sea's
voice.

Our block's sucked-dry inside went white. Like moon.

see she sly
a like move
on the sea

she she is
a move like
night-sea

Your face's hole went still. You said a lot

Crackling light stinks on a wall of tilting ragged blocks.

A fish-bit turns still
in a motionless revolution
of rock-stack. A gaseous

fossil. Wash careers through igneous creases: seals
a glistening agreement of crystals. A sound

of this is: weallsayweseeall. Seals
linger on a sizzling wet cross. An undulating

field of sea's harvest is
a zillion animals' single jizz. White skirts
of salty fluids lust
a granite's petticoat-edges of brown fields.

of things before the block out-poured. But now

She kisses him. The stones are round beneath
their feet. They nearly topple because of

the noise of sea; its uneven shifts leave
two molluscs in the cave of their shared mouths.
Shoes are useless for lovers' old beliefs
so their feet are bare but bruised by latent grief.
Only their cave & salival creatures breathe
whilst the rest of their flesh begins their deaths.

your voice is cracked & old; your sense is hot

Black-box rock. Record. Zawn.
Sea's salivating tongue going
in out cruelly like pornography.
Groin. Moist grind of pebbles.
Here's a fleshwork. Slippery bone.
Soggy skin. Salt-clogged fur.
Lost dog. Found at sea. Sea-eaten.

A carcass sniffed
by sea's vast nostril

to smelllessness,
to smellselse where,
to smells of else.

& sandy. Words are bones—so like a cow's
at roadside picked by crows.

Oedipus sees sea as:

government under water-clamour; clatter
of igneous eggs laid by ground's commission,
ratified by sea's transparent tax; green

weed's multiplicity, its shivers of dance, accounted
for in the bloody orbits of zawns.

Whilst She rips a shore into rooms r
evolv
ing no-humans, and worlds spin
across
a granite's crushed hell statements.

Yet still our block,
though split & bled blank, if touched can shock.

She is a bit turned
in a sea's petticoat-edge, in
a revolving edge

of her self, in a vulva edge

of her self. She

sleazily leases
her room to light only
by day. Seals

linger on this dark. Smells

else . . .

Noise at Gwennap Head, West Penwith

I

Gwennap Head's coastguard lookout sits
alert as an owl,
like a skull growing eye-ears.

Always tuning-in to sea,
its cross-shaped mast delicately
squeaks & clinks, its flag flaps; feeling

for something shaped-but-unsolid like words:

the one-&-million syllables
of salt-breeze.

Gwennap Head's coastguard lookout is
a little concrete ship crest
-ing the land's wave, rid
-ing the still

of where England breaks

into the frozen boil & churn
of Chair Ladder's granite & crystal froths.

Gwennap Head's coastguard lookout listens
then speaks
safety-speeches & sea-chart figures;

it's a huge radio playing
on a gold/green table
whilst the sea-blue window of a world's

room vibrates

voyage

II

. . . hot sun dries my presence;
my separateness evaporates slowly. I listen

to Gwennap Head's coastguard
relating to his radio. Sun presses

me to Gwennap's ground. In the back-
ground a combine thrums

as it cuts & threshes
granite barley; it thrums

through me. I close
my eyes. My face is a dish of heat.

A big ship slowly tears its noise
across sea's cloth. My eyes fall

through deep orange. My skull,
back, buttocks, heels & Gwennap Head's

ground merge. A me begins a voyage
of dissolving into around me through

noise. A me begins a voyage
going nowhere, now here, going

to know where

Cornwall Door

the white house on the clifftop
made of seagull
black-roof beak
glint-glass eyes
curled seagull coiling
into a square-white self-nest

the garden's wind-bent hawthorn
stood against sky
is the colour of crow-call

bloom-splintered grass slopes
to bulk-columns of granite
green-bearded

thrift is dark-pink as kiss
some seduction moves stems

the cling-curl footpath
far above the hollow-solid
of spark-coated clear blue
is thin as string

my footprints are knots
the sound of my footfalls
is small Cornwalls

some about-to-happen is unseen
on the horizon's watery hinge

honeysuckle-perfume wraps
my brain in sweet foil
the scent of sun-pressed saps

is gentle laser
engraving my cells

out over the bay
white-house fragments soar
& careen
such free white bits of strange-home
afloat on air's bright weight

with screeches
that pull

me apart peacefully

Autumn & Blood

Leaves sieve late-year air;
spent veins skeletal through red's

memories of green.
Leaves curl their thought-full

lips some million times in one
tree's world. Yellow &

    red syllables slip

from a branchy mouth's forgetting
a dream. Wind begins.

Slate-green lake-water lifts
white faces of spray surprised

by Earth's abrupt tilt.
A goose skids sideways

across sky; its honk stretched out
on storm. I stand still.

A flesh leaf settles
sensitised red between your

legs. Your gusty eyes
release the leaf of my skin.

A KINGFISHER IS

still on an ash branch. Water

moves a bird's hot blue.
A kingfisher darts

close to a canal's film. I
am pulled out of me.

A kingfisher's beak
holds a fish-spark, she has caught

a part of water.
The orange of my

hopes flies by feather & bone.
A kingfisher's speed

stretches blue across
ripple-glint, then plunges out

of sight. Hold your breath . . .

Three Men, a Boy & a Four Pound Trout

I

two men
& a boy

in a boat
on a lake

the men's
father made

the men
are brothers

and the boy
the son

of one of them

II

Uncle Russ sifts through tackle.
The sun splits sparks across water,

whilst the sky like a contained lake
is bright in his nephew's eyes.

The bloodknot is neat & tightly tied
to a little grappling hook with barbs like

prongs from a shattered star.
And the spinner is the way a boy smiles

years as sunlight twirls through

III

the slap-glug
of the lake's

wavelets
on the white

plastic boat's
hull lulls

the three males
suspended

above the
lake's weeds &

muddy bed

IV

'You'll know when it's a fish!'
Russ replies to Louis' question

about the difference

between the snagged green-gleam
of water weed & a voltage

of muscle fighting

on the end
of a faint

ly shining

tight

thin

line

V

My son yells: 'I've got one! Daddy
help me!' The rod is hot and hurts

in his hands as a zap yanks it.
Louis passes the fury to me. The line

hisses and the reel's ratchet humz.
My man's hands are his. His wishes

are tight in my wrists. I wind, and
the rod bends down

like something praying.

VI

My brother, who's the fisherman & the chef, coaches
me, a poet, on how to handle my son's hope:

'Keep the rod up! Let it run! Y'v got to wear
y' fish out! Now wind! Let it run again! keep

the line tight!'

VII

The father, who is a son, watches
as his son & his son's uncle

first touch the iridescent rainbow ghost, so

sparkling & haunted with furious life.

A pair of large hands & a pair of small hands
in the water, fumbling with the blade-bright fish.

VIII

Less than three hours from lake to stomach.
The chef slickly gutted & dressed the trout
with showman's finesse. The poet turfed
the meadow, and lit a fire at the lake's edge.

Once the meat was cooked, the boy
had to at least try the flavour of his catch.

Half a mouthful of the ghost's flesh was
enough: He tasted the pondy depth below

a lake's clear presence.

Differences of Spring

Wisteria rings her lilac-coloured scent on air.
Her smell-full petal-bells hung as sucked grapes.
Wisteria's green beams bend & wind,
While her roots wrinkle through
Our ground's dark grains unseen.

my children talk
like first bracken fronds

they warn me of spring

Spring's rain rumbles on dry stones, quickly
Casts its spatters to soak over dust. A thrush
Rushes his glisten-sounds through wet air. Sky
Sails a self across its own glossed skin.

my children talk
like rain on flowers

I want to hold each drop

Hawthorn throws her dough-like May smell.
Her white pentagrams bounce as breeze rubs.
Hawthorn's green castles of leaves shiver easy.
Green writing writhes and serrates its season.

my children's talk
simple as swallows

I listen like a lake

Own Words

I take a paper of outstretched
hand   my daughter's   I may crumple

but gently   or interlock
ink of my older fingers with

absorbing fibres of hers   hold   *hand*
is a word   is her hand a word ?   her

face is a *said*   a *say*!   yet it's there
& here   and can be   beyond &

without my gaze   without
my throat's noise of her name   she

is there / here in a sound: *Tess*   yet
outside letters   my daughter grows

she's 6 years of of-world   she can spell
many parts of   *world*   ink

of her writes-onto   writes-into
rites-through   papers of my bones

www.ingramcontent.com/pod-product-compliance
Lightning Source LLC
Chambersburg PA
CBHW031158160426
43193CB00008B/422
9781905700974